LUNAR ECLIPSE

poems

Helane Levine-Keating

Finishing Line Press
Georgetown, Kentucky

LUNAR ECLIPSE

Copyright © 2018 by Helane Levine-Keating
ISBN 978-1-63534-393-9 First Edition
All rights reserved under International and Pan-American Copyright Conventions. No part of this book may be reproduced in any manner whatsoever without written permission from the publisher, except in the case of brief quotations embodied in critical articles and reviews.

ACKNOWLEDGMENTS

I wish to thank *THE MALAHAT REVIEW* for publishing an earlier version of "Loon."

I am grateful to the Dyson College of Arts and Science of Pace University NY for awarding me a sabbatical that allowed me time to complete this chapbook.

Special thanks to Michael Braziller, Mark Hussey, Diane Keating, Charles North, Eugene Richie, and Barry Wallenstein for their thoughtful comments and encouragement

Publisher: Leah Maines
Editor: Christen Kincaid
Cover Art and Design: Helane Levine-Keating
Author Photo: Michael Braziller

Printed in the USA on acid-free paper.
Order online: www.finishinglinepress.com
also available on amazon.com

Author inquiries and mail orders:
Finishing Line Press
P. O. Box 1626
Georgetown, Kentucky 40324
U. S. A.

Table of Contents

ELEGY AT BIBÉMUS	1
CUL-DE-SAC	2
THE NATURAL THING	4
U-TURN	5
LETTING GO	6
WHO SHALL SAY WHAT IS KNOWN	7
NIGHT	8
TO KNOW THE PLACE	9
THAT SPRING	10
LATE LOVE	12
METAMORPHOSIS	13
LOON	14
COUPLETS	15
FIRE IN YOUR HAIR	16
BECAUSE	18
YOU RIVER	19
WAITING	20
LINES	21
I AM THE TRANSLATOR	22
GREEN DREAM	23
ISLAND	24
HARBOR	25
THE LANGUAGE OF BODIES	26
THESE TWO	27
MYTH	28
LULLABY	29
THE OTHER ROOM	30
LUNAR ECLIPSE	33

for Michael

ELEGY AT BIBÉMUS

> *Regardez cette Sainte Victoire! quel élan, quelle soif impèrieuse*
> *de soleil et quelle mélancolie, le soir, quand tout retombe!*
> —Paul Cézanne, 14 avril 1878

I remember it was a long time ago there was a stone table on a terrace
a laurel tree a statue of Aphrodite and a bust of the last Duchesse de
Gramont beside roses and a terracotta wall draped with trumpet vine

when the *mistral* came the air was yellow and our thoughts were dark
and edgy like a river ready to flood though the land was dry
and our shoes were dusty and hot

sometimes I could find my way to hidden gargoyles
by following the spiked scent of rosemary
but at night with the shutters fastened I was alone

by day the boy rode on your shoulders and the sea was
quiet warm and clear as my eyes are now
on a different continent so much later in the day

what I knew then I could fit in the pocket of my blouse
though I packed a large suitcase and could read a map
the name of the dog was *Flamme* and we ate slowly and well

there was a mirror and you were watching me
in the ruby room with a green velvet couch on which
I lay alone as morning burst in the windows out of breath

at noon the sun hung above us as the rasping drone of cicadas
vibrated from plane trees and Cézanne's mountain shone victoriously
shade and rest were required but we didn't speak the language

in the pitiless furnace of light everything was set in relief
yet everything was obfuscated and what I wanted then
I would want still only then I imagined I could have it

CUL-DE-SAC

now sunset flames across
the horizon framed by
river   brownstones   lick of
cobalt cashmere lidding this
crimson explosion where
two leafless trees   arms akimbo
flaunt bony silhouettes

I am walking toward the end
pearls of light beckoning
from a passing tug   a slow
barge   the opposite shore   but
I can't see Lady Liberty
outlined in red
till I reach the iron fence

she is weary tonight her lamp
dim against the backdrop
of unabashed blush   her solitude
crowded   there is no place
left to put those tired poor
she thinks though to her right
new buildings rise in curves
nowhere to make them
at home she fears despite
the generous harbor spread
round her stolid feet like a blue
tablecloth waiting to be set

across a ruthless current
she and I stare at each other
one looking east   one west
bridging evening's thickening
a tall kindly woman gazing at
me through the lowering dusk
she in relief   I in shadow

she on an island   I looking
out for her at the dead
end of this December
this darkening cul-de-sac
they call Grace Court

THE NATURAL THING

the natural thing would have been to walk away
not stay in the same position
but I wasn't sure what color I wanted the walls to be
whether there should be two walls or three
or a back door or maybe a window
instead of a fourth

for a long time I didn't mind the noise
the way it ricocheted off the wall
that was only visible from a certain angle
or how it would grow flustered and briefly break
into birdsong then return to its whine and whistle
when I couldn't make up my mind about
the other person in the room whether this
was happiness or misery or real life or
really living or flannel or linen or
granite or flagstone

how much easier would it
have been to saunter outside to pick
a dinnerplate dahlia and notice the mist
exhaling from the dew as dusk was aching
to whisper about everything awaiting me
fragile and blue yet relentlessly windy

U-TURN

everything you wanted me to know
I knew just as I knew where you hid what you
thought you didn't want me to know
though you left a trail of crumbs

the sky is glowering resembling
a scowl that crossed your face
that day when you didn't get
what you thought you wanted

such wavering sounds made by
such wanting such a plaintive
sound is I want you want
once we were wanted

it's always that way
that sudden u-turn between
what we think we want
and what we want

LETTING GO

I needed to know if it was possible to find it
but the roof leaked and I was jealous
even my own shoes didn't fit and the floor sloped

everything was always outside me
the way the gray wolf knows
to wait beyond the gate

so much had to be jettisoned to find even the outline
where there had once been an entrance
was now a sheet of ash

first I let go of nametags and the silver box they came in
then birthdays anniversaries deeds titles and the ratty mink coat
that had long been dead

I moved on to cellophane wrappings over dust-colored memories
brave attempts at scaling spiral staircases
the closet of outgrown lust sorrow and board games I never won

cut rupture breach were my talismans
as I gouged and spalled searching for the fontanel
for the lost caul that would bring good luck

too old to know the difference between right and wrong
through a scrim of rain I finally saw in the futile clearing
the secret of the door is neither in nor out

WHO SHALL SAY WHAT IS KNOWN

first a wind
but nothing shook

then sunrise
but no one saw

stars opened
and closed
like tulips
after dusk

the black
moon rose
then rose
again

again
quiet rain

NIGHT

we have come to this landscape tentatively
quietly shoeless
but not barefoot
gloveless but not ice cold

we know that hawks
slender and wide in their flight
wild as swallows and terns
descend to kill pigeons and voles

we have watched some who once were friends
turn their backs to steal
what they think is theirs
as words dissolve into spit

and we have watched our loved ones
forget that all views are skewed
depending on which side of the window
we stand and the precise time of evening or day

for the reflection changes
from moment to moment from here to there
and when night simply falls
it disappears and all we can see looking in

is the glow of a lamp through an old window
a woman or a man with a child on the lap
a small halo of light upon an open book
that struggles to speak its truth

TO KNOW THE PLACE

for the first time
she knows the place
but it is at least
three fields from where
she had expected
and the names though familiar
are pronounced with a different accent
but she can see
her way round its walls
even in darkness
and follow its scent
of overgrown lilacs
and the old woman
who once handed her
a wishbone might
well be baking marble cake
in a yellow kitchen
but an oak tree is missing
and the front door has no knob

what is beyond the slight bend
is nearly recognizable
a piano   a sofa   a wide picture window
that had once been deliberately broken
the very same books on the shelf
still in alphabetical order
but now when she reads them
though she has read them all before
it's as if she's a wizened little
wise girl happening upon them
for the first time and though
her mother is calling her
to the table for dinner
she suddenly realizes it's too late
and she doesn't have to go

THAT SPRING

I went down to the hollow
many times that spring though
the sky was still cold and flinty
the willows refusing to be green

I went back and back
but found nothing
not a footprint
or a single glove
not even a snapped twig
though I knew you'd been
there speaking to the trees
calling them by their true names
reminding them to wake up
there was work to be done

someone had dug up the ginseng
and the lady's slipper
but that may have been before
there was no way to tell

was that your nervous
hushed scent I caught when I
knelt to feel the earth's tough
winter skin soon to soften
almost ready to become
something else entirely though
the wind still flung empty vowels

I went back down to the hollow
as days lengthened like an early lily
and looked for signs of wrong weather
as if weather were ever a clue

I looked for you everywhere amongst
new ferns and fallen trunks birds
calling to each other and responding
in foreign tongues the sky
brighter than yesterday though
not at all bright not yet

I looked for you in the not yet bright
sky above unfurling ferns above
lost lady's slippers and sentries of spruce
but the sky kept rushing away
having somewhere crucial to go
belonging to someone else

LATE LOVE

with one slash into the landscape
everything shifted

precarious cairns piled
at the epicenter collapsed

molecules rearranged themselves
into invisible fractals

where light once held sway
shadows crashed into chasms

some saw the splendor of change
the lability of lines

others craved the past
nostalgia's cozy lair

yet even chaos has a rhythm
of loops   peaks   and drums

like the cadence of late love
before it's over

METAMORPHOSIS

the transition from human
to fish is not immediate
first there's the desire
to leave the air that comes
quickest when the sky is bright
the crossing from one world to another
like falling in love
the shock of current and cold
how water slides around one
with its lapping grip
the vigorous movement transforming
arms and legs into fins and tail
the ability to see under water
that gradually occurs until
the human leaves and the fish emerges
but the fish does not feel
the water any more than
humans feel air yet not
all humans were once fish
for example you I know
were once a hawk

LOON

loon's a word I've always used
calling her a loon for loving such a fly-by-night
shouting *You're crazy as a loon!* at my son
as he kicks off his shoes
heads into snow barefoot
leaving a trail of black holes

as if I knew just how crazy loons could be
as if I'd seen loons all my life
lived with them catalogued their
most secret habits knew they
couldn't walk on land
looking tipsy when they try

now listening to the loons cry
night after night outside my lakefront window
sensing it was loons I heard
that first night here
their hollow song comforting me
surrounding me like a necklace of o's
a stippled lullaby from the dawn
of my childhood

I can see that they're not crazy at all
but subtle graceful loners
who swim placidly along then dive
only to appear lengths of lake away
without a gasp without a ripple
their dark trickster bodies unafraid of day
their crippled feet swift navigators of the lower depths
the demented laughter an oracle
set to music

COUPLETS

a red latched door in the vines
opens like an eye

for a scant sigh until
a figure shuts it

someone knocks but no one answers
is it the sailor mending his net

who has dozed off and cannot
hear the woodpecker waking the tree

so does not answer the door
but what is the question really

does this carmine door swing open
or close upon their first time together

afraid to open their eyes or
feel their way across

the dark threshold
where a door opens like an eye

blinks   shuts   opens   blindly stares
yet offers a brief glimpse barely

FIRE IN YOUR HAIR

it is true there was fire in your hair
it is true the flames had no scent
although you were in grave danger you were safe
as always I worried about you
following your passage like heat after silence
like silence after smoke
you noticed no one and only turned your head
when you felt the breath of the blue heron
as its wing grazed your shoulder blade
stop was a bone in my throat

it is true there was fire in your hair
it is true the flames had no scent
as soon as I saw you I knew
doubt was a stone surrendered
though you were not expected at that dusky hour
in that mercury form or in that burnished place
I recognized the signs the way one senses
that earth which is sacred
some would say it was a dream but I knew it was not
you pronounced words cautiously
so as not to spill a drop
lightning flew

it is true there was fire in your hair
it is true the flames had no scent
it is true you walked forward then drew back
then walked forward like a man in a swamp
like a man in honed pain
although I wanted to run to you I stood still
stark in the sunlight I stood still

I waited
days passed
still I waited
then I waited once more
I was longing to put my hand in the flame
I was longing to feel the fire on my fingers
I was longing to run my fingers through flames
and my hair through firewater
I was not allowed to touch you
but I knew it was absolutely necessary

BECAUSE

because the smell of rain sneaked suddenly into the desert between us
and the damp black loamy smell of earth rose like dust between us
and the wet thirsty desire of the soil and the clay and the rock
snaked up through the fissure between us
I didn't know

the wind with its fitful flightiness was more knowable
the ocean with its brute taste for salt was more knowable
the white spiral hiding in the heart of the one calla lily was more
knowable even then

but I didn't have to know
the thin line of flat bones like a string of ancient amulets dividing
your chest answered all I needed to know and all I did not

and the trail of fingers left no mark

YOU RIVER

you river
I hold you in my hands but you will
not accept my embrace
your weight crushes me
then buoys me
dragging me under your nakedness
then kicking me forward
when I prefer to float

you river have a soft tongue
wooing me beneath the slate
gray striations of your surface
that hide an unanswerable depth
and a belly slippery as a whale
fin or a drowned sail
on a bed of washed bones

you my river
belong to no one
not even the eels that sleek past us
in a dark no one can see
not even the sky
you carry delicately in your arms
sending its blueness back into itself
not even the sun you let flay you
into glittering paths of dawn or eventide
not even the ones who ride you day after day
in their tiny toy boats with their nets and poles
not even the ones who say
you river my river
least of all
them

WAITING

the conversation waiting to begin as if we'd just left it
for a moment as if we'd always been having it
as if we were starting where we'd left off
as if we'd always been going there

many people crowding the room
your voice parting the waters of sound
asking me if I'm ready to begin
the last waltz left for us to dance

longing rises like bread
new light igniting the elm
and near the doorway to the barn
cows saunter out at dawn

LINES

I saw you and then you saw me
the black rock parting the sea glistened
you turned the corner before you looked back
night fell into our lap

who can say with a straight face this is true
the wind softened your face
where would you go if you cannot go back
wind high in the hollow

a flute made from a willow
things I know you don't know
he ate his breakfast at dinner
things I know and you don't

her back was once like a willow
things I know and you don't know you know
we buried her near the deer path where she liked to walk
things you know I don't know

the sign on the gate says the party's been cancelled
and the fireworks over forever
things you know I know
you remember what I remember

I AM THE TRANSLATOR

sniffing out words
their mercurial scent
a whiff of crushed thyme
released by heels
climbing the hill toward
the little forest
of gangly trees slowly swaying
in a henge
of furled ferns

the sound of sky
and its daily inhabitants:
clouds wind birds moon
lightning and the sun's
lusty rays   the rise
and drop of the orange oriole's
whistled octaves
the cardinal's
double spondees
briefly blazing by
like a wild poppy
surrounded by an ocean
of meadow
a white lace handkerchief
seconds after a nosebleed

the body's cadences:
insistent internal rhymes
unexpected line breaks
silence onomatopoeia space
oxymorons like similes
for all that is unassimilatable
your sudden swift beating of iambs

GREEN DREAM

> *Verde que te quiero verde.*
> *Verde viento. Verdes ramas.*
> *El barco sobre la mar*
> *y el caballo en la montaña.*
> —Federico García Lorca, Romance Sonámbulo

do you remember the green dream of nights without frost
that came in the morning of one eye open
found the door and entered gently
with a porcelain cup of tea

such a wooing dream of honesty spoken
after the lights were out
all the kind words stored up neatly folded
and vertically stacked in the bottom drawer

do you remember the sky kept changing
its mind about what it could still hope for
before the meteors rushed by stealing
all its stars and thunder

wait you said you heard someone at the door
but I said no it is only the wind
kissing the window and you whispered
you must be kidding

before the dream said follow me
I know the way
and you told me you agreed
so I followed until

someone invisible said
there will be a sign on the door
you will know it when you see it
and only then will it be obvious

where we are going
how long it will take
and exactly why green

ISLAND

now that you've come to the island
you can smell the smoke on the leaves
and see the outline of sheep in the last
gold light and the crimson dewlap of wild turkeys
poking at their feet you who have never
walked these shores as a girl can feel
sea stones and pebbles cut your toes
though he said the beauty is worth it
the sun loose in the dark red water

the souls of those who once fished
and swam will be invisible to you
he said nor can you hear
the faint song of my childhood playing
on an old guitar
but look
there across the sound
soaring wide and high
flickering above the herons
yes right this minute
look
two hawks

HARBOR

the small night moves in
closing doors and shutters
but not before the faces
peer in at yellow
lamplight beside the fireplace
and the photograph taken
long before you were born

as I hold you in the night
you dream of a safe harbor
and a bookstore and I
I sleep lightly
one ear to the wind
making certain the waves
keep their distance

sleep I say to you quiet
beside me in the night
turning to hold me in
half-light telling me
the story of your dream
holding me this once
before the faces vanish
and the image fades

THE LANGUAGE OF BODIES

the language of bodies does not use words
speaks in sentences of arched
cadences that can never be repeated
even in a whisper
can never be translated into
another language
can only be understood
by one other body without a name
who replies with movements
that rise subside and rub against
other movements
like fish parting a stream

the language of bodies weaves a conversation
no one else can hear
saying how all that has come before
means nothing
opening a door while
closing another as fingers shape
meaningless words dependent on
the rhythm of breath that rises
then subsides like a storm or a breeze
yet always returns to
what has been left unsaid

THESE TWO

after I dream of meeting you
when we were both young
the you in that square kodak photo
dark-haired long-haired
brow uncreased
the me in bell-bottom hiphuggers
long-haired blonde-haired
hands on hips
grinning with their whole lives
opening before them

they crawl into bed with us
waking us in the middle of the night
steamy and insistent
kicking off the sheets
insinuating themselves into each caress
as if they had always been there
nibbling biting ripping grabbing
urging us to fly
in the face of caution

last night I saw his smile on your face
this morning you glimpsed her eyes in mine
yet now in the quiet dusty afternoon
they've suddenly disappeared
but maybe they'll return tonight
breaking and entering
like the thieves they are
determined to rob us of our years
resolved to become us
yet taunting us
away from the cave of old hearts

MYTH

it took a long time for us to travel through the forest
brambles and thorns had to be pried away
fallen leaves were slick with dew
a clutch of stories wild with despair
was jettisoned in autumn so we could
keep our focus on the snow ahead
large drifts made it hard to find each other
and we took turns sucking icicles
though our hearts were blue and old
until we warmed our fingers in body fire
but once the days grew longer and lighter
and the wandering sun gazed at us aslant
and bears slowly awoke   scratched   roamed
our dreams turned red then orange then black and
a full moon rose fast over the last hill
then one star and another and another

LULLABY

and it's too late for me to go to sleep
think of all I'd miss as stars vanish
the moon sets
and birds begin to waken

if it's still dark
how can you tell it's dawn
sneaking into your warm arms
but what else could it be
so filled with raw newness
that never could have happened before

kiss me
everyone says
as dawn does its work

kiss me
I say
as dawn draws near

kiss me
when it's almost here

THE OTHER ROOM

1
in the other room time is a word
no one knows how to pronounce and
the skylight wears its rain lightly

nearly morning
the hard double bed
the cobalt walls
the song of the cardinal
mourning doves cooing

they brush against each other
like branches across a stream
of melting ice and mallards
trout hidden in shadows
and water rushing downhill
breathlessly

2
in the other room a man
is stroking a woman's knee
like silken hands along a silken leg
a bow slides across the cello
and it's morning or winter
caverns canyons
a hollow wind or
a screech owl's cry

ancient finger prints
whispering their story
curled shells flung far
across damp sand

3
in the other room
the sly moon vanishes
then reappears quite alone
only the sound of satin and quiet

the faint smell of dusk on eyelids

the door is opened
night enters
slowly
as if it were merely
a summer afternoon

4
in the other room

where you want to be
other than what you are

where you go to uncover
exactly what
the other one already knows

where a skylight
stares at setting stars

and dawn always rises alone

5
nothing between them
but space and words
shadows and rags
of other lives
flickering through walls
passing through eyes
she said
there are no other lives
in the other room
only this

and this only
for which there are
no words

6
he said

do not go
I will take you to
my other room
for the first time
this is given to you
an offering
an altar
an hour
of awe

this is given to you

open your arms
now

7
sleeping alone
in the other room
indelibly flavored
by slivers of apart

but some nights
the other room
falls off the outline
of life's map

both of them
together and alone
like music
then silence

her hand softly waking
the small of his back

LUNAR ECLIPSE

night first slow then fast then slow again
the sun starting high then sliding quietly
while weeks pass and still we're watching
until everything speeds up
as suddenly it splashes
large and naked and red-bottomed into
the black-rust sea then stripes of blue and orange
and cardinal gliding across the sky
like Rothkos slowly shapeshifting
and me lighting a candle
while a cold white moon creeps up into
the sea-black sky until fast now faster
warm breath on my thigh
as it bursts into its fullness
at the very top of the sky and just hangs there
teasing glowing red-bitten vanishing
then returning hours later
with its cool-warm light when
right before dawn
as the green buoy chants its forlorn
soothing it slips
out of the almost night-less sky
briefly hovering in its rapture
before roundly plunging
as soon we will
into a silver triangle
of dawn-lit sea

Helane Levine-Keating was born in Brooklyn and grew up on Long Island, NY. After receiving her B.A. in Comparative Literature and Creative Writing from the University of Rochester, she completed an M.A. in French Literature at New York University, and a PhD in Comparative Literature from New York University and the University of Paris in 1980 and studied creative writing with Anthony Hecht, Sharon Olds, Galway Kinnell, Edward Field, and M.L. Rosenthal. A professor of Comparative Literature and Creative Writing at Pace University New York since 1983, she divides her time between Manhattan and her home in the Central Catskill Mountains in New York. Her poetry has appeared in numerous journals and anthologies, including *The New York Quarterly, The Malahat Review, Women and Stepfamilies* (Temple U Press), *Heresies, Facere, Graham House Review, Central Park* and *Like Light* (Bright Hill Press). She is the co-editor of three editions of *Lives Through Literature: A Thematic Anthology* (Prentice-Hall/Pearson). Awards include an Academy of American Poetry Prize and the First Anaïs Nin Memorial Prize at NYU. Besides contributing essays and book reviews to *American Book Review, The Woolf Studies Annual, 3 Quarks Daily,* and other journals, her fine art photography has appeared in recent solo and group shows in various galleries in the Catskill Mountains, New York City, and Vero Beach, FL.

www.ingramcontent.com/pod-product-compliance
Lightning Source LLC
LaVergne TN
LVHW041555070426
835507LV00011B/1104